UNDERSTANDING

YOUR
3 YEAR-OLD

UNDERSTANDING

YOUR
3 YEAR-OLD

Judith Trowell

Warwick Publishing
Toronto   Los Angeles

ISBN 1-894020-03-0

Published by:
Warwick Publishing Inc., 388 King Street East, Toronto, Ontario M5V 1K2
Warwick Publishing Inc., 1424 N. Highland Avenue, Los Angeles, CA 90027

Distributed by:
Firefly Books Ltd., 3680 Victoria Park Avenue, Willowdale, Ontario M2H 3K1

First published in Great Britain in 1993 by:
Rosendale Press Ltd.
Premier House
10 Greycoat Place
London SW1P 1SB

Design: Diane Farenick

Printed and bound in Canada

49.1

Parenting

CONTENTS

TAVISTOCK CLINIC

The Tavistock Clinic, London, was founded in 1920, in order to meet the needs of people whose lives had been disrupted by the First World War. Today, it is still committed to understanding people's needs though, of course, times and people have changed. Now, as well as working with adults and adolescents, the Tavistock Clinic has a large department for children and families. This offers help to parents who are finding the challenging task of bringing up their children daunting and has, therefore, a wide experience of children of all ages. It is firmly committed to early intervention in the inevitable problems that arise as children grow up, and to the view that if difficulties are caught early enough, parents are the best people to help their children with them.

Professional Staff of the Clinic were, therefore, pleased to be able to contribute to this series of books to describe the ordinary development of children, to help in spotting the growing pains and to provide ways that parents might think about their children's growth.

INTRODUCTION

This book is about the 36- to 48-month period of your child's life. This is the time when a child usually begins some group activity, joins a play group or starts nursery school and enjoys playing with other children. Younger children play alongside each other in the sandbox, riding small tricycles, doing puzzles, but until about three they find it hard to play with other children for any length of time. By this is meant jointly deciding to build a tower, play racing cars and then race them, build a fort and then play a story in it, or be together in the playhouse. So the child of this age is venturing out into the world and for periods of time may be separated from the person they know best, their mother or father, and is also making friends, having close emotional contact with adults and children outside the family.

Alongside this, children are developing very rapidly in most other areas but may at times appear to stop or even go backwards. For instance, most children have gone through toilet training and have learned to be clean and dry, but there may still be accidents. The three year-olds enjoy physical activity, running, climbing, riding tricycles, most enjoy wading pools and water play and a few may be swimming. When they have appeared to learn how to do something, they can seem to go briefly into reverse and become very reluctant to try, then climbing or swimming may be avoided for a while as though they suddenly see the dangers and lose confidence.

Generally the three year-old will have a loving relationship with Mother, but it is not unusual for this to be a time when a new baby arrives, which means the three year-old may also have to learn to share. So three year-olds who have developed a strong sense of who they are and know that there is a loving, caring mother who is there to look after them, now find this mother has someone else to look after and think about as well as our three year-old. Temper tantrums are common. What these mean, why the three year-old can sometimes be very grown-up and at other times like a little baby will have to be understood and talked about by the parents so that they can think of ways of managing their child.

Three year-olds are curious, find the world great fun, endlessly exciting, and obtain enormous pleasure from the new relationships outside the family with both friends of their own age and outside grown-ups. They also frequently have colds, coughs, earaches, and the common infections they catch at play group, so that caring for fractious children is also part of the three-year-old world. They are a great delight but can also be very tiring, so it is important to be able to enjoy the good times and have someone to help, give a little relief, in the bad times.

CHAPTER ONE

MILESTONES AND CHANGES

Language

Most children have learned to use the toilet by their third birthday, although some are well into their fourth year before they master this. Many three year-olds are very anxious in case they have an "accident" and in new strange situations may become flustered and need to be tactfully helped to find the toilet and assisted with awkward zippers or buttons.

With the confidence that comes from this mastery, there is energy released and what seems to blossom for three year-olds is language; many will appear to talk endlessly, asking questions, making comments and giving detailed accounts of what they have seen, done or imagined.

Susan aged just three followed her mother around asking one question after another. "When are we going to the park?" "When is Granddad coming over?" "When will the rain stop so we can go out?" "When can Jane [next door] come and play?" "When is it time for TV?"

After the TV program Susan played with her blocks, making a house for her toy rabbit, and told the rabbit in detail almost exactly what had happened on the show, which then became a long story of her own. Susan's mother, who overheard this, was surprised at the detail of her account of the program but then amazed at the story Susan wove around this. By the time it was done, the rain had stopped and they could go out to the park. Susan chatted steadily all the way there, while there and then all the way back, about the grass, the trees, the flowers, the cars, the people, the dogs, the stores—everything was of interest.

This shows how delightful is a child's curiosity, interest and enthusiasm, but also how demanding these verbal children can be. Other children are shy and do not speak so easily.

One boy of three and a half worried his nursery school teacher because he never spoke to any children or any grown-ups. His mother was puzzled since at home he chattered away to her, his stepfather and big sister. They were new to the area and James had only been in the nursery school for a short time. Four months later he was talking up a storm to the other children but was still reluctant to speak to grown-ups outside the home.

Some of the shy, quiet children can take time and require patience. It is hard sometimes not to become irritated or impatient with them, but, given encouragement rather than punishment, they usually slowly become more forthcoming.

Some children do have difficulty with speech; this may be the practical actions that need to be carried out by their mouths—B's and P's— and with encouragement this can be overcome. Using the lips and tongue to form the letters clearly and hence produce the sounds may need to be repeatedly shown to these children. Other children have problems with the second half of a word, saying "by" for bike, "co" for coat. These children are in between, still using baby talk but also using adult words more as the year goes by. They also need encouragement and as much talking to, and with, adults as possible.

Most children really delight in having stories read to them but, in addition to this, they need someone who will talk to them and follow their lead. So that when a child says "by" for bike, the reply is, "Yes this is your bike, you want to ride your bike." A good way to encourage a child to talk is through sharing a TV show just seen, for instance: "What happened next?" "What color was the car?" "What did the bunny rabbit have to eat next?" "Why don't you tell me what adventure Teddy had next?" The more the child is encouraged, the more lively and fun it becomes.

Drawing and painting

Three year-olds have a great time with paints. They love finger painting but also enjoy using a brush and pots of colors and begin to develop shapes and figures, simple houses and people and scenes, the sea, the sky, hills. What is important is to be pleased and proud and to let your child know you really want them to tell you about their picture.

A mother gazed at a colorful but apparently rather vague creation, but when her daughter Emma began to talk about it, there was a rainbow, a monster, a witch and a house with a princess. There then followed a story about how the rainbow's magic drove the witch away and the princess was happy in her house and garden and flowers appeared.

As well as holding a big paint brush, three year-olds can hold crayons and felt-tip pens, so hours can be spent drawing shapes, patterns and pictures. Colors and shapes, circles, squares, and triangles can be drawn, but the main interest is in making pictures which have to be admired and talked about. The child of three draws or paints familiar things—my house, that's me, Mom and Dad. They also create pretend scenes and can become very caught up in these, which may be happy or exciting but may be very scary, with frightening witches or monsters. Your child often urgently needs to tell someone close to them what it is all about. It is very helpful to take drawings or paintings seriously, as your child wanting to share something, and to try and make the time to hear about them.

Physical developments

Your three year-old will delight in physical activity. But they do tire and it is important to stop them getting over-tired and exhausted. So a burst of physical activity can be followed by storytime, or watching TV or a video for a little while and then another time for physical activity.

Three year-olds are rapidly learning new things. They love singing and dancing games and can develop real skills at clapping, stamping, dancing to the rhythm or singing simple songs. Nursery rhymes are obvious examples but there are other simple songs with a clear beat and easy melody that three year-olds can greatly enjoy. They can march up and down, perform simple actions so that they are learning co-ordination of feet, hands, body and head. They also enjoy making music; banging drums and cymbals, shaking rattles, playing triangles and bells and tooting on a whistle can be great fun for a group of children or, where there is one child, joining in when the music is on a cassette or disc. Saucepan lids make good cymbals.

Three year-olds also love riding their bikes, using climbers, slides and swings. They need to be kept secure with safe surfaces under the apparatus, but managing themselves is a good challenge as long as there is a watching adult. Similarly, many three year-olds find enormous pleasure in water, in summer in a wading pool or water, and throughout the year in a swimming pool.

Margaret Green was new in the area and her son Jonathan seemed so full of energy that she found keeping him occupied exhausting. She saw a local swimming pool advertising sessions for mothers and under-fives and went along. Jonathan, three and a half, loved the water and paddled around with water wings. Mrs. Green met another mother and as they stood in the water they chatted. The water was warm and Jonathan wanted to stay longer but, with a promise to return, they left after thirty minutes in the water. Several weeks later, Jonathan and Mrs. Green went swimming twice a week and they were both much more relaxed and content. Jonathan was tired and relaxed after the swims and they both enjoyed an outing together which they could look forward to, as well as meeting the new friends they had made.

The changing view of the world

Your three year-old has to make sense of lots of new things. But perhaps the biggest thing to sort out is what is real, what is actually happening or has happened, what is "pretend" from a story or TV program, and what did I just make up out of my own head. Of course the three year-old doesn't understand all this, but it is important for the grown-ups to know they are often struggling and may be uncertain, for example about witches or monsters. Grown-ups also play a part in this make-believe with Santa Claus and the Tooth Fairy.

Sarah told her mommy there had been a fairy at play group who had given her a candy. Her mother was puzzled. Sarah had been in a bad mood the day before because she wanted candy and Mom had said no. Mrs. Brown decided Sarah was still cross about the "no candy" decision and had comforted herself with the pretend fairy who gave out sweets. Sarah insisted she had indeed had a candy from a fairy. Mrs. Brown asked more about the fairy. Sarah described a nice lady who told them she was a good fairy that protected them and whispered in their ear, "Don't run in the road." The lady had come to the play group and they had practiced not running into the road, waiting for Mommy or a grown-up and going across at the crosswalk, and then they had all been given a sweet. When they went to the mall that afternoon, Mrs. Brown met a neighbor and learned there had indeed been a road safety visit to the play group.

Sarah could have made it up, but in fact it was real. Other times children recount things with complete conviction which then turn out to be untrue.

John told his mom that Wendy's dad had died. He was quite insistent. Mrs. Smith became very concerned and John remained convinced because Wendy had told him. Mrs. Smith remembered that when John last went there to play, Wendy's dad had told John off for trampling on his new plants in the garden so she thought that John might wish Wendy's dad wasn't there. Finally, Mrs. Smith telephoned to inquire carefully. Wendy's dad had had an anesthetic to have teeth out and had been "asleep" for a rather long time. Wendy had reported her dad had gone to sleep and couldn't wake up. John remembered Granddad who recently died and they had talked about his long rest, sleeping in the sky. The confusion was explained, but what followed was a time to talk about sleeping, dying and being put to sleep to stop bad pain.

Changes of mood

Sam woke up at 6:30 am, crying and upset. His mother came in after a little while when he was crying vigorously and he screamed to see her. She sat on his bed and held out her hands and arms to hold him. He shrank away but as she remained there, he moved to be hugged by her but he hit her and kept repeating, "Scary Mommy, Mommy hate me." His mother tried hard, she held him, stroked him and talked to him. He talked about Mommy hitting him, Mommy hurting him, bad Mommy. His mother remembered that a few days ago he had been about to put his hand in the electric slicer and she had grabbed him, with the result that he had slipped off the top of the kitchen counter and briefly he had been suspended by her hold on his arm. He had been shocked, frightened and hurt by her grip on his arm. She asked about dreaming, but he could only repeat, "Mommy hurt me." Slowly he calmed down and they explored together where he hurt and found all was well. Sam was ready to get up, so they went downstairs for some cereal and a drink. Soon Sam was eating up, talking and asking what they would do that day. By 9 am Sam was busy playing on his bike, talking to the dog and full of the joys of being alive. His mother, drained and tired, wondered if she would make it through the day.

Your three year-old changes moods rapidly and dramatically. The feelings are very intense but they pass. A small thing may be felt to be a catastrophe, their world falls to pieces, what appears to be a small change in plan, a small frustration, a blue pen instead of a purple pen, chocolate chip instead of peanut butter cookies, and the child can be in a rage. But then other small things appear to have no impact. A parent, anxious about how to introduce a change, finds it is accepted and their child moves on to something new with no problem. A child's reaction or mood cannot always be accurately predicted, which makes understanding their responses always interesting and surprising. Even when you feel sure you know, something different can happen.

Three year-olds have sensations from their bodies—a tummyache, a cold, feeling hot and achy, a pain in their foot. They also have sensations which are reactions: "Mommy said no I can't watch TV or go to play with Eduardo," or "Yes we will go to the park and visit Jenny." They also have sensations which are reactions to thoughts and feelings in their mind. "I'm frightened, the curtain moved, there might be a witch in the room, I'm excited because we are going to Granny's but I can't wait." All of these will produce effects and the three year-old is often unclear what they are feeling and what comes from where. So for the adult it is often difficult to know how to respond. If the child is distressed or angry, this can be very hard, because until they can sort out what it all means, what it is about, little can be done to help. Excited, happy children will usually talk easily; unhappy children may become silent. Some angry children shout, others hit out, slam, bang doors, run to their room or run away. The important thing for the parent or adult is to find a way of helping the child put their feelings into words, so that the child, and the adult, can understand what was happening, what it all meant, even if nothing can be done to change it.

CHAPTER TWO

YOUR THREE YEAR-OLD
AND THE FAMILY

Anne arrived at play group and told the new helper, "That was one of my mommies. I have two mommies and two daddies." The helper gulped and said, "Tell me about them." She learned that this three year-old with her elder brother spent Monday, Tuesday and part of Wednesday with her Mommy and new daddy and the rest of Wednesday, Thursday and Friday with her Daddy and new mommy. Alternate weekends were spent with each.

Nowadays, almost one in two marriages end in divorce. Many children have to live with different family arrangements. It is helpful and important for the three year-old to be clear on what is happening, where they will be sleeping, where their toys and clothes are; it may be that they have two sets, one in each household.

Laura lived with her mom, she did not know who her dad was, but she knew Mom's brother, her granddad and grandma and her cousins. She asked about her dad and was sad when Mom told her the oft-repeated story of how he had gone away to work, had met a new lady and had a new family. She often looked at his photo and wished he would come. "When will my daddy come?" she used to say, but now she did not because Mom used to keep crying. But she was also a bit glad he did not come, because this way she had Mom to herself; lots of her friends in nursery school had only a mom or only a dad. She thought it was OK. This is what Laura told the nursery assistant who asked about her family.

Ricardo, her nursery friend, told the nursery assistant that his mommy was big and strong and went to work to get the money. His dad was not well in a special chair with wheels and he was at home and made dinner when they got home.

Joshua said his mom was at home and she must do the housework and make the dinner, his dad was very busy with so much work and they all had to be very quiet at home so as not to disturb him.

Three year-olds have to learn that there are lots of different sorts of families. They start by thinking every family is the same as theirs, but once in play group, nursery school or daycare they soon hear about all different types of families. They can feel upset, puzzled or jealous— why isn't their family like that? The mother or father, the adult, has to listen to their complaints and questions, such as "Why do I get fewer presents, have fewer toys, not so many grandparents," and then try to help their child understand all these different arrangements.

The three year-old needs to know who will be there, that they are loved and wanted, that they matter, that they are safe and can trust the adults to do what they say. They have to talk about the good things and bad things, about having a mommy and daddy together, about having just a mommy or just a daddy or about having a new mommy or a new daddy. Three year-olds often are unsure what to call such new parents; "Mommy Jean" and "Mommy Susan" may feel all right. Sometimes they decide on Mommy, and the new mommy is called by her first name. All of this takes time to talk about, but there are often very powerful feelings which can cause distress.

Your three year-old also knows not only that there are boys and girls but also that the skins of children are different colors.

Rachel came home from play group and said there was a new boy who was different. Her mother asked all sorts of questions to try and understand; he wasn't like John, Rachel's special friend; no he wasn't like Jesse, Jesse had black skin and very curly hair; no he wasn't like Ahmed who had brown skin and black hair. Rachel's mother was unsure what to think, when Rachel announced that he had shown everyone that he had one blue and one brown eye. They talked about this and Rachel said she thought one blue eye and one brown eye was just as much different as black or brown skin. Her mother had to think hard to follow as Rachel went on to say how at play group they all played and what she did was play with people she liked.

It is not easy to allow our children to be in the world which is different from the world of our own childhood. They meet a range of skin colors, different religions, different styles of clothes, different ways of looking after children. They need to talk about it, taste the tastes, smell the smells of different foods, learn about how their friends' families live, and they need to be able to come home and talk to their own family about it. They will continue comparing, this is how my family does it but their family does it differently, eats different foods, goes to a different church.

Parents often find it confusing and can be worried that their child will lose his or her particular identity, culture or religion. It is hard sometimes not to be frightened or angry, but if it can be seen as an exciting adventure, a voyage of discovery with the likely outcome of a return to base, then it can be exciting to see the possibility of hope. As children get to know each other and each other's families, the chances increase of liking each other, accepting each other and in time reducing fear between families, fear of the unknown.

Three year-olds may also meet for the first time others with a disability. They may have met blindness or deafness in a grandparent, but now there may be other children who have a disability at the play group.

Peter told his mother about this boy from another country but couldn't explain why he was different. He also tried to say the boy, William, didn't run around with them, didn't speak to them. His mother couldn't make sense of this and Peter was obviously bothered, so his mother spoke to a helper. Peter's mother was told, "William has Down's syndrome." Peter's mother and father and Peter talked about it later and Peter wanted to give William one of his toys. Peter decided that he and his friends would invite William to come and play with them. Some weeks later, William was part of the group and joined in their play and their games.

Young children, three year-olds, are acutely observant. They notice differences—boy, girl, skin color—but as these examples show, they also notice disability, that other children are physically or mentally different. However, unlike adults, they are usually not afraid and can be very curious. But they can more easily satisfy their curiosity. So three year-olds want to look, touch, say things out loud. This can lead to embarrassment on the part of adults and may lead to distress in the disabled child. It is important in a calm, simple way to explain what the child can and can't do. As with Peter, his parents were able to talk about William's areas of difficulty. Fear comes from not understanding, not knowing what is going on, why there are differences, and fear is also transmitted to children by adults. Peter could have been told to avoid William, to keep away, given the idea that the difficulties were somehow catching. Luckily for Peter and helpfully for William, Peter's parents explained and talked to Peter so that he saw William as a person, a boy with his own personality, able to do some things and not able to do others.

Brothers and sisters

If the three year-old is the last in a family, this can feel really good. Simon said, "I am special, my mommy didn't need any more babies after me." As the youngest child, they may indeed be special and this can be a very privileged existence. The only difficulty is that Simon, when he got to nursery school, was very sad for a while when the teacher did not spend her time with him. He wanted to take her a present because, he thought, then she would like him best. Simon cried when he had to wait his turn and found sharing crayons hard. His mother was worried, but when she talked to the teacher they agreed Simon had been really lucky with his sister of 9 years and his brother of 11 years. He needed lots of loving and hugs at the end of his time in nursery school, but Mom also needed to explain that when the teacher was busy with the other children it did not mean he had misbehaved or been forgotten. She told Simon that when he needed help he could get it, but in between he played with the other boys and girls. Simon slowly found it easier to be there, to take his turn and to share.

Jacky was three and a half, her mother had a little boy, Christoff, just over one year, and now she was pregnant again. Jacky had often been angry at daycare, hitting other children. Her mother was puzzled— Jacky was so sensible and grown-up at home. Her mother explained that if she asked Jacky to fetch something she was very good and did so. If her brother was crying in his crib and Mom had gone to sleep in the afternoon, Jacky went and sat with her brother and talked to him and played passing toys through the crib bars. Seeing them together at the clinic, Jacky was busy helping Mom, passing her things, smiling at her. When Jacky did a drawing, she drew her family including her baby brother and mother's fat tummy, then stabbed at her drawing with the crayon. Jacky was now able to talk about how cross she felt at her brother and the new baby. She shouted at both her parents and said angrily, "Why is there a baby in your tummy, why don't you send it away, we have Christoff, I have to help with him, there will be too much to do with another baby." During a long talk about Jacky and how she felt pushed out, the little girl Jacky that wanted to be cuddled and babied climbed on to her mother and had a hug. After this meeting, Jacky stopped hitting the other children but also sometimes shouted at Christoff, telling him to be quiet, not to make all that noise.

Mark was really excited; his mommy had a new baby in her tummy and the baby was coming soon. Dad was excited, Mom just seemed to want it all over now. When the new baby arrived, Mark rushed to tell everyone. He seemed enormously proud of his baby sister. He showed everyone the new car she had bought him. She was going to have his crib and he was having a new big bed, he was delighted. Some weeks later, he had become more realistic. This sister was OK, she did cry a lot and feed a lot, she kept Mom busy and she was no good for playing with, she had better hurry up and grow and start to move soon. Mark found it hard to imagine a long time like months or years before she could play with him.

All these children have had to cope with the issues of sharing. The only child or children with much older brothers or sisters can avoid sharing early on, but once they start meeting with other children regularly, it is an inevitable lesson to be learned. Generally, children with brothers and sisters are forced to share. It can be quite painful, it can be difficult, but with sensitivity it can be negotiated. A three year-old will get cross from time to time. "Why do I have to let her have a turn, let her sit on your lap, let her have my chair?" But given time and reassurance that they are still loved and wanted, that they are sharing, not being pushed out, then, with patience, the three year-old settles down to the new order.

Separations: Going to sleep away

Diana was full of excitement. She was going to spend the night with her special friend, Barbara. She was going there to sleep. She knew the house well and the bunk beds where they would be sleeping. Next day at the daycare she talked of sleeping over at Barbara's and what fun it had been, but she had been really glad to see Mommy in the morning. Diana at 3½ years had stayed with her grandma and Aunt Sarah and now she had slept over at her friend's.

Diana's mother was building up a number of familiar places where Diana could happily go and sleep over. This meant that sometimes Diana slept out when her parents went out, but also that, if for some reason Diana's mother had to be away suddenly or for a longer time, there were places where Diana could go happily and easily. Diana's paternal grandmother was frail and there was a strong possibility that Diana's mother might have to go and help in an emergency. Mother was also hoping to have a new baby and so she wanted to prepare Diana for any separations that might need to be negotiated.

Three-year-old children are able to cope with separations if they are prepared. When they are warned in advance and there is a background of trust in their parents, they believe they will tell them the truth. For instance, it is especially important that adults come back at the time when they said they would. Parents should not use threats of going away or sending a child away because however the child reacts outwardly, inside they can become very anxious. This uncertainty and anxiety inside can alter the way the child behaves, whether they will trust other human beings, or whether they will be constantly wary and suspicious.

Hospitals

If your child has to go into hospital, and you want help over preparation, there are a number of nice picture books that present the necessary information in storybook form. Three year-olds can understand this quite well, but the pain of injections and the pain when waking up, for example after a tonsillectomy or hernia repair, can still be very distressing. It helps a child to be told but not terrified by the information they are given. Having a parent or loved one there can make the pain bearable. Children have amazing resilience and recover very rapidly. They can be directed and distracted by toys and play materials. The most important influence on the child comes from their parent. If the adult is calm and confident that all will be well, the child can draw on this strength. If the parent is very anxious, the child senses this and becomes even more anxious themselves. So an important aspect of going to hospital with your child is to find out as much as you can, so as a parent you are prepared and will not be shocked or shaken by what happens, and then telling your child what they need to know without playing it down or being too frightening.

If it is the parent who has to go into hospital, the child will need preparation in terms of what will happen, who will look after them, where they will sleep. It will be important, where possible, for the child to visit the person in hospital. The mother ill, pale and tired in the hospital bed can be very frightening, so the child needs to be prepared. If there might be assorted tubes, this needs to be explained. Children are very adaptable; the important thing for them is the emotional tone, the way the adults react.

Stephen's mother went into hospital to have her wisdom teeth removed. Stephen's granny came to stay and he thought this was a lot of fun. His big brother had teeth missing, he knew that they fell out, but his mom had to go into hospital so they could cut out some of her teeth. He went to visit his mother the next day and was quite subdued. Mom looked funny. Her face was all swollen, she didn't say much and she looked pale and miserable. His dad had told him Mommy felt hurt, and he wondered, why did they do this to her? Yet two days later he was cheerful again. Mom was home but Granny still looked after him and made the meals. Mommy was resting. He was a bit cross with all this resting but he could play with his friends so it was OK.

If longer hospital admissions occur, it helps to be as straightforward as possible, perhaps to explain that it is not certain yet how long it will last, but that the doctors and nurses are doing everything they can to make Mommy or Daddy better as soon as possible.

Back to work

A more major upheaval in the family is when a parent, usually the mother, decides to return to work. This may mean more money for treats or it may be income that is needed to keep the household afloat. Both parents are likely to be more busy and to have less time to spare, so the three year-old may find that the amount of attention they receive goes down considerably. Childcare arrangements can vary. One parent may be able to take and pick up the child from daycare or nursery school. If both parents are working full time, a substitute caregiver may be needed. This may be a family member or a family friend, or it may be a business arrangement with a paid babysitter. This is a very common arrangement these days, with the habit of extended families living close together becoming less frequent than it used to be.

Cindy came to daycare and told the other children that today her mommy would not be picking her up, Mrs. Brown would come. Suddenly she looked sad. A helper sat on a chair and Cindy climbed on her lap for a cuddle. Cindy said they needed money for a new car, their old one kept stopping, and they needed money for a holiday in the summer. The helper said, "But right now I think you want your mommy." Cindy looked solemn but then she brightened and said, "Mommy will come later and I can play with Sean till then." (Sean was another child at daycare, the son of Mrs. Brown). This conversation was repeated several times over a period of days and then Cindy seemed to settle into a routine.

CHAPTER THREE

YOUR THREE YEAR-OLD IN THE OUTSIDE WORLD

There are a number of ways in which the behavior of the three year-old can make life easier or more difficult outside the family. But the patterns are set inside the family, they fall into five broad categories.

Anger and temper tantrums
Fears and nightmares
Independence
Sleeping and feeding
Toilet training

Anger and temper tantrums

Three year-olds get angry, adults, parents get angry. It is quite normal but there is an impression that it is wrong to become angry. This means that it is very difficult to think about ways of being angry that are not dangerous or embarrassing. If we can all accept or understand that we all become angry, then it is much less difficult. The difference between children and adults when they become angry is that adults, parents, hopefully have thought about what to do when they get very cross and annoyed. They have thought about being firm and clear and definite but not going over the top, not losing control. They have thought about ways of avoiding going too far, like walking out of the room, going out into the yard, walking the dog, or just going into another room and watching TV, putting on the radio or music. Children, three year-olds, have not done all this thinking; when they get angry it is there on the surface, expressed for all to see.

Tom, just three, lay on the floor in the supermarket, kicking and screaming. his mother had a large shopping cart full of groceries and Tom's baby sister perched up on the cart seat. Tom's mother became more and more upset and angry, there was nothing she could say to Tom to stop him. He wanted a large expensive toy and she had said no. She felt guilty and embarrassed, they could not afford the toy. Passers-by in the supermarket aisle looked at them. Some were understanding and compassionate but more seemed to look accusingly—"What on earth have you done to the child?" Tom's mother grabbed him by the arm, yanked him to his feet and half pushed him to the checkout. He sobbed and yelled steadily. As they walked to their car to unload the cart, Tom's mother lost her temper and began to shout at Tom and she hit him. Someone at a nearby car came over and helped get Tom and his sister into their car seats while their mother unloaded the cart.

Recounting this story, it emerged that Tom was angry more often recently. There were more temper tantrums. The situation at home was stressful. The baby was six months old and Tom's parents were having many disturbed nights with her teething. There were also financial problems and so Tom's parents were tense and worried. Going shopping was a difficult time, seeing all the possible purchases and facing the money shortage. Yet both parents felt they went without themselves to give to their child. Tom was seen as greedy.

Tom's mother thought about other ways to cope. If shopping was a tense time for her, she could she help herself by leaving the children with a friend or relative, since managing them was a handful. Tom's mother decided that during the big shopping she could leave Tom and his sister with their father, but she also thought that to make an outing of going to the mall for a few items with the children would be all right. Her anger and tiredness could be thought about and, when she felt relaxed, Tom could be talked about and discussed. Later, Tom's mother talked with Tom about how much he wanted things and how hard it was when Mom said no. They also talked about his tantrums when he got so angry he didn't know what to do. His mom told him she could keep him safe even if he hated her now and then, since there would still be times when she would have to say no to him.

Children do have outbursts but they need the grown-ups to be strong, calm and firm. When they are not, the children become frightened. They need to be angry and to know the adults can stand it and survive. Adults also can get angry and this is good for children to see, when the adults are angry but also have ways of managing it.

Hannah was crying, upset because her toy rabbit had lost an ear and her mother could not mend it. She started to shout and pull at her mother to stop what she was doing in order to come and try to mend the fluffy rabbit. Her mother, tired, was trying to get the evening meal. She realized she was getting angry. She took Hannah and put on a video that Hannah liked. She then went out onto the balcony for a few moments to pick off the dead heads from the geraniums. Feeling calmer, she returned to the vegetables and when the saucepans were on she went over to Hannah. Hannah was engrossed in the video and came to her mother's lap. They hugged and Mrs. Green told Hannah, "We were both tired and hungry. When we have eaten we will look at your rabbit and see what I can do." Hannah smiled, "Mommy was angry"— "Yes, I was angry but it's better now."

Going to another room, out into the yard, for a walk, or next door to a neighbor, or a diversion to another activity, reading, watching TV or a video, are all good strategies for managing anger. Temper tantrums in a three year-old can be worrying and frightening. If the child really does seem out of control, it can be helpful to pick them up, hold them or put them on their bed until they calm down.

Linked with this is the issue of discipline. Children need to be firmly told "No" and they need to know adults mean what they say and will stick with it. So it can be very helpful if the parents or adults looking after children have similar views. If the parents do not agree, it is important that they decide, in advance, how they want to manage particular situations, and whose view will be acted upon. It is very unhelpful if each parent says different things and they end up arguing.

Beth was picked up from daycare by her granny. Mother had returned to work because of financial pressures and so Granny cared for Beth until her mother came to get her on the way home. Beth's mother was very concerned about nutrition and wanted Beth to avoid eating sweet things to protect her teeth and to stop Beth putting on weight. Granny thought that there was no harm in a few candies at lunch time to settle Beth down for the afternoon. On weekends Beth pestered her mother for candy and this ended up in angry tears, sometimes on both sides. Beth's mother needed her own mother's help but felt furious at her wishes being disregarded in this way. In the end Beth was spanked quite hard by her mother for demanding sweets. Beth's mother realized she needed to talk to her own mother because Beth was being given mixed messages. They managed to agree on a few sweets after lunch and both spoke to Beth about this.

Discipline is important. Children need to learn what they can and can't do. But it is sensible to consider the number of rules and decide on the important ones. When they break some of these, it can be useful for everyone to know the hierarchy of punishments. First "No," with the expectation that the child will stop, then "time out" in their room, then stopping something nice or longed for, e.g., watching a certain program, an outing to the park, a new toy or special treat to eat. It is better, if possible, not to hit a child, but it does happen and when it does it is a good idea to talk it over afterwards. "You were behaving badly and Mommy got angry and hit you. I'm sorry I hit you, I do love you but I didn't like what you were doing and lost my temper."

Simon came into his nursery class and announced, "My mommy did hit me."

"Oh," said his teacher, taking a deep breath, "what had you done?"

"I hit our baby on the head with a hammer—real hammer," said Simon.

"You must have been angry," said his teacher.

"Yes," said Simon, "angry with baby and angry with my mom."

"Why were you angry?" asked the teacher.

"Mom was talking to baby and feeding her."

"So you hit her?" said the teacher.

"Yes" said Simon, "and my mom hit me, she was angry with me."

This followed a situation in which Simon's mother had managed to sort out with Simon that he was angry and she was angry, but that the hitting that had happened had been wrong.

There are times when physical punishment can be important. If a child is about to run out into the road in front of a car, or about to put a hand on a hot stove or is up on a window sill when the window is open and they could fall out, then it is vital to grab the child physically, by the arm, the shoulders, or whatever is necessary, which can cause pain or bruising. A child's safety needs to be addressed first and at such times there is no point in asking or telling a child what to do when they are only a few seconds from danger.

Fears and nightmares

Three year-olds can be full of themselves—they know everything, can do everything, the problem is just the adults who restrict them. But at other times they can be very shy and frightened. Going to a strange place, meeting strange people, can for no obvious reason leave then very scared and timid. Sometimes, as well as the strangeness, they are so involved in pretend play or fantasy and imagination that they lose sight of what is real and what is not.

Greta came into the playroom and began to play busily, putting all the animals in families. Suddenly there was a breeze and the curtain moved. Greta jumped. "Who is there?" she asked. When asked who she thought it was, she said, "The witch, she keeps coming after me in my bedroom and now she is here." When asked what the witch might do, Greta said, "She might take me away." Greta had recently had to spend a week in a foster family while her father was working abroad and her mother had to go abruptly into hospital for her appendix to be removed and there was no one to care for her. Greta had become frightened and timid after this. Fortunately, Greta could talk of her fears and anger but she still remained shy and anxious for some time.

James was in trouble at nursery school because he kept hitting the other children. When he was asked about it, he couldn't explain it at all. Sitting watching James, it was interesting to see what happened. He would approach a child to try and join in a game, the child would turn away and then James wandered off looking miserable. When two children playing together started to laugh, James went over and hit them. When he was asked, "Why did you hit them?" he didn't know. But when asked, "Did you think they were laughing at you?" he said, "Yes."

Children react differently when afraid. Greta could talk about her fears, James could not, he just did something. It is useful to find a way of putting fears into words so that children can make sense of what is happening and find ways to manage themselves, perhaps by talking to a grown-up or, by the time they are nearly four, by talking to each other.

Three year-olds can be very afraid of real things, for example going swimming, sobbing at having to get into that pool of water, or being left behind. Sometimes even having to go somewhere familiar like play school may just be too much. It may be that the child is a bit unwell— a cold coming or a sore throat, but it may be just a feeling that it is all too much and today they just can't face it. Letting up for a while on all the activities or arrangements to go and play, may provide just the space the child needs to bounce back.

Nightmares can be very frightening for parents and children. If a child wakes, sobbing and terrified, it can be difficult to comfort them as they may react with fear of the adult until fully awake. If the parent has struggled awake and out of their bed, a frightened, hostile child can be difficult to manage; the child needs to be held, even if there is resistance or fear, and slowly the child will come around. If a child then becomes very clingy and difficult to settle, sensitive but firm handling may be needed when the moment feels right to leave.

Three year-olds may be able to describe their dreams or nightmares but some cannot. Michelle said, "Monster eat me up." Damien said, "Daddy chasing me with a big stick." Mary said, "Don't know," and started to cry and said she was frightened. If your child can talk about their nightmare, it is important to listen patiently even though you are wanting to get back to bed yourself. Nightmares usually mean that a child is worried or upset about something, so it can be helpful to spend time in the day with your child to try and understand what may be causing distress.

Independence

Independence is an area that raises many questions. Children need to be encouraged to take responsibility for simple things, to carry messages, to be seen as competent. However, it is important to recognize that their capacities are limited. children forget, become diverted, get lost or confused. Accomplishing small tasks within their competence gives three year-olds great pleasure. Sadly, it is generally not safe to allow children to go out alone, but with an adult they can help choose items from shelves, handle small amounts of money and help unload purchases and put them away. Much more important is encouraging independence in terms of their own body and needs. Some three year-olds begin to take themselves to the toilet to urinate but they may need help with clothes. Three year-olds are usually keen to feed themselves, to have a say in their choice of food and their clothes. Most children quickly learn to turn the TV and VCR on and off, but it is important that the parents decide what are appropriate programs and what are not. Children should not be allowed to see any program or video merely because it is there. Allowing your child to gradually do more for themselves is not easy. It is often so much quicker and safer to do it oneself. But three year-olds need to take some risks under supervision, they need challenges to learn new skills. Three years old is when it all begins.

There are well-known struggles with children of this age but that doesn't mean that when confronted by them one knows how to react. More usually there are a number of options in general use and the parent feels bewildered. Should they do what they think, what the book says or what a range of relatives say?

The most important and sensible approach is to do what feels comfortable for you and that you can see through confidently, but to remember to give yourself time to think calmly. It is vital in these difficult situations not to react instantly; take time to consider.

Mandy was a bright, confident little girl who would soon be four. She was determined to wear whatever she wanted to daycare and would also get a chair, open the front door and set off to walk there in the mornings on her own. Mandy's mother often felt very angry when

Mandy insisted on wearing her best clothes to daycare and then come back covered in paint and glue. She also felt angry at having to rush out and either follow Mandy to daycare or have a scene and drag Mandy back home in order to leave at a more suitable time.

Mandy used to wake early and she would go and choose what to wear herself. Mandy's mother decided to change this. She shut the closet securely, having first chosen herself two possible outfits. Mandy could choose between these two. This worked well and Mandy seemed pleased, she still chose what to wear. The fights over clothes diminished. Mandy's mother also decided to lock the front door so that it could not be opened before she and Mandy were ready to go out. Mandy became very angry at this and kicked the door and raged. After three mornings of this, Mandy played with her toys, asking Mom from time to time when were they going. Once the front door was open, she ran off, but looked back to check that her mother was coming and waited at the roadside until her mother said it was all right before racing across.

Peter kept having fights about going to bed. He would be in the middle of a very intense game, or engrossed in a video or TV program. It was never possible to get him to bed smoothly and peacefully. His parents decided to have a talk about it. Peter said he wanted to say for himself when he went to bed—perhaps when they went to bed. His parents said no, he was only three and three quarters and needed more sleep. They decided that after supper, before he became busy again, they should decide together the right time for bed. They could decide on the TV programs and agree where the hands would be on the clock when he had to go to bed. Peter was initially cross, but all the same this plan was followed regularly. He was part of the discussion and could say what he really wanted to do, or what TV program he wanted to watch, and the time was set to try and fit in with this. Peter soon settled into the new routine and mostly the time would come to go to bed and he would go up cheerfully.

Sleeping

Getting your three year-old into bed is one thing, sleeping is another. Most three year-olds are so busy all day, they sleep soundly through the night. Apart from those already discussed who have nightmares, there are children who can't get to sleep, others who wake very early and others who seem wide awake at two o'clock in the morning. Sleep disturbance is generally a phase, the risk is that it will settle into a routine. Children need to be encouraged to remain in their room. They can play but it is not a time for being up and about and all over the house. If the child gets thirsty, a drink by their bed can help; if the child needs to go to the bathroom, then this should be as easily accessible as possible.

Julie woke every morning at about 6 am. She was alert and bright, needed to go to the bathroom and then was set to begin her day. She had toys by her bed and a cassette player with her story tapes. With these she would be content until 6:45 when her parents' alarm went for the start of their day. She was always very keen to recount the story on the tape while her parents dressed.

Daniel went to bed at about 8 PM. He had gone off to sleep in minutes for weeks, but one day, after a fight between his parents, he lay in his bed for a while and then kept coming downstairs. That night this seemed fair enough; his parents understood that he was perhaps checking that they were both there and all right. But this pattern went on for another two weeks. Daniel's parents talked together about how worrying their fight must have been. They then explained to Daniel that they knew their threats to leave must have made him scared, but this was not really going to happen. They had both been angry and upset. So now Daniel did not need to check they were still there. If either of them was going off anywhere or was going to be home late they would tell him. They went on to talk about how they might help him to stay in his bedroom and settle down quickly. Daniel said he would like a night light again and they agreed to this. They talked about cuddly toys. Daniel asked to have a story tape when they left after his bedtime story. His mom and dad agreed to try this. That evening, Daniel went to bed after his story was read, the story tape was put on, the hall light was left on and his door left open. Twenty minutes later, his father looked in and Daniel was sound asleep.

Difficulty in getting to sleep or early waking can be an intractable problem, but it is helpful to see it as unlikely to continue indefinitely. The important thing is to keep the assumption of a reasonably regular sleep pattern alive and calmly try to encourage your child to stick to a routine.

Feeding

Three year-olds generally eat anything and everything. Given the chance, they will fill up on cookies and sweets, so some regulation is needed.

The most common difficulty is the child who is seen as a faddy eater, a picker. It may be that the child is never really hungry because of ready access to sweets or cookies but some children really are small eaters. They may need small, more frequent meals. Some children find certain foods difficult; fish, eggs and green vegetables, except peas, are generally unpopular, but worth trying in small amounts.

Linda was just three when she went with her mother and father on a long drive to stay with her daddy's parents, her grandparents. They lived three hundred miles away and had not seen Linda since she was six months old. They were very excited, as was Linda. But the drive was very long and by the time Linda arrived she was exhausted. Granny had made a lovely meal for them all and Linda's mom and dad were delighted. No one noticed Linda much, they were so busy talking. They had lamb chops and were busy eating. Linda poked the chop, pushed it around, tried to pick one up and bit it but the hard bone hurt her teeth. Finally, she threw it onto the floor. Granny's dog immediately devoured it. Linda began to sob, the adults looked around and it was a few moments before they realized what had happened. Linda was given more meat from another chop but refused to eat it. She finally ate a fish finger and went off to bed. It was some weeks before Linda could be persuaded to try the meat from a lamb chop again, she just cried whenever she saw one.

Scott would never eat his meal when it was put in front of him, he just sat and messed it around his plate. He was a slight boy but lively and vigorous, so there were not any serious concerns. His mother knew he loved to visit the old lady next door and he had started going in there often. He went through a gap in the hedge and she was always pleased to see him. Scott was nearly four and was in nursery school. He used to go next door when he came home before he was given his main meal. His mother became curious and decided to go with him one day. In the next-door kitchen was a little table and chair and on the table was a neat pile of four cookies and a package of jelly beans. Scott went straight to the table, sat and ate everything and turned as he was offered a beaker of orange juice to wash it all down. His mother felt angry; her prepared meal would again be wasted. But she was also aware of the old lady's delight, her pleasure in Scott's visits. Scott's mother decided to say nothing, to think about it. She suggested that their next-door neighbor might like to come and visit them. Then she would see Scott's baby sister as well and some days Scott could have his meal at home first and go next door afterwards. These changes seemed to work well and when Scott went after his meal, his mother noticed he often took a book with him. Scott explained they were reading stories together today. His mother smiled and gave him a new book from the library to take.

Sometimes children are so faddy that they really are not eating enough and lose weight. This is worrying and it would be sensible to consult your family doctor. If a child is eating unusual things, such as dirt, it would be wise to seek advice.

Toilet training

Most children of three years are clean and dry, but they may easily have accidents. If a child is still wetting or soiling, it can be very distressing or embarrassing but, if possible, it helps just to change the child into clean things and then get on with other activities. If the child has never been clean or dry or both, then it might be sensible to take advice. Many children develop control later, some children not gaining full control till five or six years or even later. This can often run in families and seems to be a delay in normal development that just means the child is a bit behind in this area.

Matthew, three and a half, was upset—he had wet his pants again. The other children called him smelly at play group and laughed. The play group leader told his mother that Matthew was upset. His mother decided to see their general practitioner, who tested the urine and said there was nothing to worry about. Matthew's mother, when asked, remembered her husband and his brother were both slow to become dry, as her mother-in-law had joked about it only a month ago. The doctor agreed it could happen in families and they must wait and hope. Matthew was almost five when he stopped wetting. He told his mom, "Now it just seems easy to go to the bathroom, I can go when I need to do it." He was very proud of himself

If a child is dry and then becomes wet or dirty again, it can help to try and understand what happened when there was the relapse. Often there is no apparent reason but sometimes it can be the arrival of a new baby, the death of a grandparent, or perhaps the parents have had a big fight. Starting nursery school may also be a cause. Children may be upset but often find it hard to talk about.

Melanie's mom had a new baby which was adopted. Melanie and her big brother knew her mom and dad had chosen another baby because they wanted to look after a baby and there were lots of babies with no one to love and care for them. At first Melanie thought the baby was all right, but soon she was crawling everywhere, Melanie's toys were moved and her games spoiled. Melanie began to wet, although she had been dry for nearly a year. She was very clear when asked about it. "Mommy is very busy with Sophie, feeding her, putting on clean diapers. When I'm wet Mommy comes to me, puts on clean pants and talks to me, she is not with Sophie." Melanie's mom decided to spend time every day reading Melanie a story and the wetting settled.

Some children wet or soil and nothing seems to help or change it. Parents can feel very angry, upset and helpless. Sometimes it can feel as though the child is almost doing it to make their parents feel humiliated and a failure. If it really does feel as though the situation has become so tense and full of conflict that there is a real risk of one or other parent losing their temper with the child, then it could be helpful to seek advice.

All these activities build on three-year-old development, but now the three year-old spends more time outside the home, parents feel other adults can really see how they have done as parents. They can feel tense and judged, seen as a success or failure depending on how their child behaves. This feeling is picked up by the child and they may behave especially well, but it may not work out well at all and the child, feeling tense and anxious, may have some temper tantrums, be more fearful or clingy, may be more difficult over eating, or wet or soil themselves more than usual.

If their parents are relaxed and confident, then usually children respond to this and cope well. Whatever happens, it is important to prepare your child, to give encouragement and praise and, if possible, laugh and shrug off any lapses. If a child feels valued and loved, they want to try their best and please their parent, even if it doesn't always seem so at the time.

CHAPTER FOUR

PLAY

Play is what young children do most of the day and often they are envied, seen as having no problems, no responsibilities, just able to spend all day playing. Is it really like that? Well it may appear to be play but in reality there are a number of purposes and a range of activities.

Play can be a solitary, individual activity, or it can be alongside others, as with three year-olds when they keep a watchful eye on each other but rarely play together. Children of this age may co-operate by taking turns on the swing or slide, or they may share, for example the sandbox or water tray. By the end of the third year, children can really play with each other to some extent, sharing toys, games and even ideas. Play can be divided into a number of activities and each has its contribution to make to the life of most children. But perhaps one of the most important things about play is the real, yet not real, world into which children can escape.

CHAPTER I

The Mole never heard a word he (Rat) was saying. Absorbed in the new life he was entering upon, intoxicated with the sparkle, the ripple, the scents and the sounds and the sunlight he trailed a paw in the water and dreamed long waking dreams.

CHAPTER VII

But Mole stood still a moment, held in thought. As one awakened suddenly from a beautiful dream, who struggles to recall it and can capture nothing but a dim sense of the beauty of it, the beauty. Till that too fades away in its turn and the dreamer bitterly accepts the hard cold waking and all its penalties, so Mole, after struggling with his memory for a brief space, shook his head sadly and followed the Rat.

The Wind in the Willows

The Winds in the Willows is the story of an imaginary world and in it Mole at times has dreams, pretends, imagines, until he is unsure what is real and what is not, and neither is the reader.

Children love having stories read to them and gradually acquiring the skill themselves. Depending on its content, the material can be educational, imitative, creative or involve fantasy. The spoken word encourages children to develop their own imagination to pretend the scenes, the people, the noises, sights and smells, and this capacity is an enormous asset. Radio and tapes are similar but do not have the intimacy of being read to by a loved person. Of course, children spend long periods watching television and videos. This, too, can be educational, imitative, creative and involve fantasy. But the creativity and fantasy are second-hand, the pretend stories come from the mind of the writer, they do not arise or spring from the child's mind and therefore may not do so much to encourage their development. A child can learn much, but to depend on television or video leaves the child as a recipient, not a participant, other than some participation in another's world as a spectator.

Dean's parents were worried because he spent so much time watching TV and videotapes, he talked about the characters as though they were real people. They lived in a highrise on the 22nd floor and there was little space to play, apart from in their small apartment. At three and a half, Dean was given a place in the nursery school. Dean and his parents were quite anxious, but by the end of the first week Dean was lively and excited. He chatted to his parents about his new friends and talked endlessly and in detail about all the games he played, monsters, witches and dragons were everywhere. He was also very proud each day as he brought home a painting, a construction or a cut-out picture. He was very active repeating at home what he had done with cardboard boxes and tubes and paper and colors. The toys that had been ignored in his room suddenly were important, as were pads of paper, crayons and all the household boxes. Worries about Dean evaporated; he was now too busy and spent much less time watching TV and videos.

All children need imitative play when they can play out, sometimes repeatedly, events in real life or from stories, their dreams and imaginings. Mommys and daddys, hospitals, schools, the latest craze in TV cartoons, superheroes—this play is important for children as they try out different outcomes and are able to talk to other children or other adults about what is happening.

Creative play is essential for all children. They enjoy splashing with finger paints, mud, sand and a range of other toys or household objects. They can use cardboard boxes, tables and blankets, to make forts and their own houses.

Creative play can move easily into fantasy play. Children need to escape into a world which is not governed by reality or by the rational. Fantasy play is when children play out what they have imagined for themselves. When playing in this way, a world of pretend, of myths and legend it is as though they have one foot in each and are in a special space in between. In this space children become immersed in their world of fantasy. It is important for children to have this space to explore themselves and their imagination. But they need time to leave this play. Children need to be warned that they have five or ten more minutes, so that they have time to withdraw and return to the rational real world. In some ways this play is akin to dreaming and to daydreams.

Another very frequent activity is educational play, something that parents and group settings encourage especially. Children must be stimulated and stretched, but they do also need time to relax. For three year-olds Look and Do toys, such as shape boxes, threading beads, rods with thread and nuts, decreasing barrels and hammer pegs all encourage the use of eyes and hands. Construction toys, such as Duplo, Lego, large plastic or wooden building blocks and some of the Lego sets that need to be assembled in sequence, encourage mastery of co-ordination and a child's capacity to plan and anticipate. Other toys are for thinking and doing, to encourage the child to recognize shapes, similarities and differences. These include complex shape boxes, simple jigsaws, picture dominoes, and make and do activities like play dough and cutting and pasting.

Halima was busy with the building blocks, with which she made a big tower. Her brother, Rashid, knocked it down. He was five years old and bigger than she. Halima nearly cried but took the Duplo and began to make a house. Her brother took the play dough and began to make models of figures. Halima made a house with walls, a roof and two rooms. They put in the figures, when Mark, a three year-old from next door came in. He had some Disney figures from his trip to Disneyland, and Mickey Mouse, Minnie and Pluto moved into the house. They counted the figures, four Disney ones and three play dough. Counting up to seven was a bit hard for Halima and Mark but Rashid was eager to teach them. They then went over the colors of each figure, and all the children joined in this. By now the house was forgotten, the pile of picture dominoes nearby was divided up and they all busily tried to match up the pictures. When their mother came in to say snacktime, the children, tired and hungry, rushed through to the kitchen. Looking around the room, the range of toys and activities that the children had experienced, if looked at in detail, was highly complex. It could all be described as play, which indeed it was, but each phase was a different learning experience and a different aspect of each child's personality was developed.

These different play activities can occur when a child is playing alone or in a group. At a play group a three and a half year-old child starts some imitative play. She is the mommy and she tells off her baby, a doll, "You have been a bad baby. Why didn't you eat your nice food?" Another child comes up and wants to join in. This child becomes the baby and the doll is discarded. Another child also wants to play, becomes the other parent and the three start to play house. "Let's go out for a picnic," says one and produces the tea set. Another of the children wants to go to the playhouse and play cooking. It would depend on what happens next whether the play remains as imitative or whether the children develop it more creatively.

Some of the children at a play group decide to have a picnic. This starts as a tea party but one of the children involves "My Little Pony" characters and another has various of the turtle characters join in. The children then become engrossed in a game of good guys—all the pony and turtle characters—and bad guys. There are attacks, fights and adventures, during which characters are captured and rescued. More of the children in the play group join in and play different parts, although the baddies are all imaginary.

This has now become fantasy play, with the children using their imaginations. The play grew out of imitative and creative play, which the children have used to develop their own ideas, drawing on their own imagination for the events and story. The children play different roles; at times the girls are female characters and at times they are male characters. Likewise, the boys play male and female parts. So both boys and girls have different experiences in this pretend world which they develop together.

These shifts and developments in play can be seen both when children play alone and when they play in groups. The group play involves sharing, negotiating the different parts each will play and co-operating together to create a mutually enjoyable playtime. This is another aspect of play activity, learning about socialization, getting on with each other, which is a spin-off from play. The children learn that they can have a different time, which may be more fun in a group or with another child, rather than on their own.

This is also an example of how much you can learn about your child by taking the time just to be there and watching. Often care-givers feel they need to encourage play activities, make suggestions, or organize the play. Children may need ideas at the start, but once they have begun they usually develop their own ideas and the play flows. Children can move spontaneously from one form of play to another. It is fascinating to watch and see how much you can learn about your child and yourself by just sitting quietly in a corner and allowing them to play.

CHAPTER FIVE

Some Interesting Questions

Pets

"Mommy, I want a dog/or a cat/or a rabbit." What can a parent say to a three year-old. "No" is rather brusque, "Yes" is often impossible—or is it? Of course, it will depend on many things, the living space available and the time the adults have, but perhaps most important, whether the mother or father themselves want a pet.

It can be very helpful, interesting and fun for a child, a three year-old, to have a pet. They can learn about being responsible, remembering to feed or exercise a pet. They can learn about clearing up mess, cleaning the hutch, the cage, or the cat litter.

Susie went on about a dog. Her parents felt guilty but they could not cope with a dog in their small house. Also her father worked long hours and Mother worked part-time. Susie was sad; she was an only child. They wanted to respond and so bought a hamster in a cage. All went well for a few weeks, then one morning when they came down, there was the hamster on its back, feet in the air, dead. Susie's mother and father used this (as have many other parents) to talk about dying, that everyone dies sooner or later and it is very sad for the people left behind. Susie found it hard. She wondered who would die next and was the hamster all right in heaven? When would they die? Would Granny die like Granddad? But very soon she was back wanting another pet.

Susie's parents wondered about a dog, but decided, no, it really was impossible to look after a dog. Finally they decided on a rabbit. The dwarf rabbit, black and white, won all their hearts. He seemed content in his hutch and very cuddly and liked being stroked and didn't have too many accidents. Susie did not like cleaning out the hutch, but did regularly feed the rabbit and play and stroke him. They all seemed pleased with this compromise.

Holidays/strange places

John asked his mom, "Where are we going on holiday? Everyone else is going away." His mom explained that last year they hadn't been away so, yes, this year they were going away. John became very excited.

It is not easy to know when it is best to prepare a child for the holiday. Too soon and they forget and it comes as a shock or they can become very tense and anxious, too late and they are not ready for the upheaval. Holidays away are great fun but also very stressful.

Cameron, nearly four years, on returning home said, "Phew, I'm glad to be home. My own things, my own bed—that's good."

Whether the journey is in a car for two hours or six hours by train, boat or airplane, there is always a great deal of planning, preparation and work.

To take three year-olds away, there needs to be lots of luggage, clothes, toys and some food just in case. A holiday visiting the family sounds simpler, but there will be strange beds, people sharing rooms with other family members and, almost certainly, different food. Abroad, the food, the water and the climate are all different. Three year-olds love adventures—going on holiday is an adventure. But they also get tired, so by the time the journey is over they are often exhausted and may cry, scream, demand to go home or just find it all too much and be beside themselves. It is hard in these circumstances for the adults, the parents, to feel it is all worthwhile. Hopefully by next morning all will be well, but it may take a few days. A strange bed, a strange room and perhaps strange noises nearby may mean the three year-old and the parents sleep badly despite being weary.

Journeys can be made part of the holiday. High-speed travel these day aims to get people there fast. Highways, high-speed trains and air travel all need to be treated with respect and prepared for, knowing that the unexpected will almost certainly happen. So take small bite-size pieces of food, small sandwiches, small tomatoes, pieces of carrot, perhaps bananas or apples and, of course, plenty of snack foods and cookies. Drinks and sweets are needed endlessly, but chocolate is messy and leaves children thirsty. Raisins, grapes and other similar items can be a treat. Three year-olds strapped in their seats need constant diversions. Games can help or small drawing pads and little packets of crayons. Hopefully, some of the time they sleep.

Three year-olds are often taken aback by new places. City kids can find the country difficult; cows, sheep and horses can be scary. Country children are often overwhelmed by big cities, the noise, the traffic and the people. For example, coming to a large city and traveling on the subway can be exciting, but can also be terrifying.

Jane, three, traveled across the North Atlantic. The journey to the airport went smoothly and the wait at the airport wasn't too difficult, with lots of drawings, drinks and bites of food. Walking onto the plane, there were some bad moments, the roar of the jet engines and the high-pitched whine were painful but quickly overcome. Settled in the aircraft seat, there were few problems. The flight attendants were helpful and a little pack of goodies arrived. Eating, sleeping and playing, the time passed. Arriving was difficult, earache and a bumpy descent produced tears and screams, but then they were out of the plane. However, the long stand in line to get through customs was very stressful, everyone was tired and ratty and movement seemed slow. Jane's parents were tired and were carrying Jane and she became heavier and heavier, but she was too tired to walk. When they were out and on the bus to the hotel she fell asleep. On arrival there was a flurry of activity and although she soon keeled over, the night was very disruptive. It took the next day and another night before Jane could recover her equilibrium.

Her friend, Keith, had meanwhile gone to Mexico. The journey had been easier, but he was struggling with the hot sun, the sand, the ocean and all the people. He took time to adjust.

Comforters

"Mommy, why does the lady at daycare keep telling me to take my thumb out of my mouth?" or, "Mommy, why can't I take blanky [special blanket] to play group with me?"

Most children need some form of comfort. Some may use things unseen, e.g., their tongue inside their mouth. But most frequently a blanket or piece of cloth, often something of Mother's, is used. This is lovingly held, smelled and caressed and provides security, confidence and comfort. It may be rather unpleasant to adults—dirty and smelly—but washing it is a crime that may produce considerable distress in the child. If this object is lost, it may be disastrous.

Christine went with her parents to visit Granny and Poppa, a journey of about one and a half hours in the car. She took with her Bluey—a piece of blue blanket with silk ribbon along the edge. All went well, she managed the journey there and the time of the visit, despite many strange adults and children. Towards evening she fell asleep on the couch and when it was time to leave was carried into the car. When she was nearly home she began to sob for Bluey. The blanket had been forgotten. She was inconsolable. Back home the parents debated and phoned the grandparents. With enormous difficulty they calmed Christine and next day her father and grandfather drove to the mid-point to meet and hand over the blue blanket.

Similarly, thumbs can be used and they cannot be lost. The problem with thumbs is that they can be sucked for long periods and giving them up can be a problem. Some children seem to become so attached to their thumb-sucking that they do not join in with the other children. Often they seem to be unaware that they are sucking their thumb again. Most children give up thumb-sucking, but at three years of age it is very hard to force a child to do so. Encouragement and diversions can be tried, but very often the thumb goes in when the child is tired or going off to sleep.

Pacifiers are often a worry. Hopefully, the three year-old will leave it at home under the pillow for night time. A pacifier used frequently in the day can cause worry. Gentle removal can be helpful and if the child needs it when unwell or very tired, that can be accepted. Sometimes it can help the child to be firm and remove the pacifier, at least during the day. The child's need must be thought about: why is the pacifier so important, or is it just habit?

Awkward questions: Boys and girls

"Why am I a boy, Daddy?" or "Why am I a girl?" "Can I make babies like Mommy?" Boys and girls seem to know very early that they are a boy or a girl and by three years most children are clear. However, what that means can be unclear.

Shirine said to her mom, "I'm a girl like you aren't I? You are having a baby. I have a baby in my tummy." Her mother agreed she was indeed a girl, but she, Mommy, was a woman and so could be a mother and have a baby in her tummy; Shirine had the place inside her for babies to grow but at present she was too little and couldn't grow babies. She had to wait until she was bigger.

Marc asked his mom if he could grow a baby in his tummy like Shirine's mommy. His mother explained that he couldn't grow babies in his tummy but one day he could make babies with a woman. She told him that when Shirine was bigger she could make babies in her tummy. Marc asked if his penis could make babies. His mom nodded and said yes, when he was bigger, but perhaps sometimes he wanted to make babies with Shirine or with her or with Daddy. Marc nodded and said yes he did. His mom said that she could understand that, as Marc loved mom and dad lots and wanted to make babies with them both and that it felt very sad that he couldn't. But one day when he was bigger he could make babies with girls or women, maybe like Shirine when she was older.

Divorce and separation

Mark went off to play and returned with Kate. He told his mother that Kate's mom and dad had decided not to be together, they were separating. "Oh dear," said his mom. "Kate must feel sad." Kate said they kept fighting. "My mom says it will be better, now, she and Dad won't fight any more and I can still see Dad lots."

One half of marriages end in divorce and many of these breakdowns involve children. If a three year-old is involved, they will be distressed, but if it can be handled well and the child continues regular frequent contact with both parents, it need not be too damaging to the child. Most damage is done by constant arguing, fighting between the adults and drawing the child in to take sides. The three year-old will also be distressed if they have to move or change their group of friends, and clearly if there are financial problems and their main caregiver must now work full-time and the three year-old has to be babysat, then these disruptions can be hard to manage.

Sadly, as part of such a separation or in other circumstances, there may be questions about inappropriate sexual contact between adults and children. Much has been reported about child sexual abuse. Many adults feel anxious and nervous now about bathing, changing and cleaning their child. Three year-olds can be delightful, pretty and enchanting. They can be very conscious of their bodies and how they look, especially around adults, hoping for a response. Of course adults respond. What is important is that the adults who may feel warm and loving towards the child and sometimes have sexual feelings, do not do anything to show these sexual feelings. The adults must deal with themselves and keep the child safe. So perhaps it is better not to bathe with your three year-old if you are worried or cuddle them too tightly or too often. But of course adults must show their love and affection, and children need this. The important thing to remember is that the contact must be for the child's sake and the adult must be sensitive to the child's wishes and needs. All these questions of separation are awkward. They also stir up many feelings in the adults, the parents. Parents may need to talk to their partner or a close friend to help them respond in a way that makes sense to the child. Telling the child too much is unhelpful. Not replying leaves the child bewildered and confused. Simple responses, simple answers are usually obvious, but so hard to think of when your child asks suddenly. It is important to take time to think and if need be to come back to the child to talk some more.

Conclusion

All three year-olds are endearing and exhausting. Their energy is prodigious, their needs intense, their involvement and passion are a precious gift that quickly moves on to be less intense and to be shared with others. It is important to try to free yourself and enjoy your child during this phase, knowing it will pass all too quickly. Living at such a pitch looks as though it will last for ever, when each week seems such a long time; but that is an

illusion and the demands of the outside world and school will come all too soon. Withstanding the battering and enjoying the good times brings rewards. There will be crises, illnesses, when it feels as though the world has collapsed or it is all too much, but then, as though the sun is suddenly shining, it will be all over, forgotten, as you both move on to another new experience, the next adventure.

FURTHER READING

The Making and Breaking of Affectional Bonds, John Bowlby, Tavistock Publications, London, 1979

Playing and Reality, D. W. Winnicott, Tavistock Publications, London, 1971

Child's Talk, J. S. Bruner, Norton, 1983

The Magic Years, S. Fraiberg, Methuen, 1968

The Child, the Family and the Outside World, D. W. Winnicott, Penguin Books 1964

THE AUTHOR

After working with children who were physically unwell and then for five years as a general practitioner, Dr. Judith Trowell became a child psychiatrist and child analyst. She started the Marilyn Monroe Children's Fund to provide family centers for troubled children and their families and is chairperson of Young Minds, the organization that seeks to promote the mental health of children, young people and their families. Among her many publications, she is co-author, with a lawyer, of *Children's Welfare and the Law* (Sage Publications). She works in the Child and Family Department of the Tavistock Clinic. Dr. Trowell is married and has two grown up children.

UNDERSTANDING YOUR CHILD
TITLES IN THIS SERIES

UNDERSTANDING YOUR BABY	by Lisa Miller
UNDERSTANDING YOUR 1 YEAR-OLD	by Deborah Steiner
UNDERSTANDING YOUR 2 YEAR-OLD	by Susan Reid
UNDERSTANDING YOUR 3 YEAR-OLD	by Judith Trowell
UNDERSTANDING YOUR 4 YEAR-OLD	by Lisa Miller
UNDERSTANDING YOUR 5 YEAR-OLD	by Lesley Holditch
UNDERSTANDING YOUR 6 YEAR-OLD	by Deborah Steiner
UNDERSTANDING YOUR 7 YEAR-OLD	by Elsie Osborne
UNDERSTANDING YOUR 8 YEAR-OLD	by Lisa Miller
UNDERSTANDING YOUR 9 YEAR-OLD	by Dora Lush
UNDERSTANDING YOUR 10 YEAR-OLD	by Jonathan Bradley
UNDERSTANDING YOUR 11 YEAR-OLD	by Eileen Orford
UNDERSTANDING YOUR 12-14 YEAR-OLDS	by Margot Waddell
UNDERSTANDING YOUR 15-17 YEAR-OLDS	by Jonathan Bradley & Hélène Dubinsky
UNDERSTANDING YOUR 18-20 YEAR-OLDS	by Gianna Williams
UNDERSTANDING YOUR HANDICAPPED CHILD	by Valerie Sinason

Price per volume: $8.95 + $2.00 for shipping and handling

Please send your name, address and total amount to:

WARWICK PUBLISHING INC.
388 KING STREET WEST • SUITE 111
TORONTO, ONTARIO M5V 1K2